What to say and When to say it

CAPTIONS BY BILL MARTIN JR.
CARTOONS BY BOB SHEIN

 HOLT, RINEHART AND WINSTON, INC. NEW YORK, TORONTO, LONDON, SYDNEY

COPYRIGHT © 1970 BY HOLT, RINEHART AND WINSTON, INC. • PUBLISHED SIMULTANEOUSLY IN CANADA • LIBRARY OF CONGRESS CATALOG NUMBER: 77-115045 • PRINTED IN THE UNITED STATES OF AMERICA • ALL RIGHTS RESERVED. PERMISSION MUST BE SECURED FOR BROADCASTING, TAPE RECORDING, MECHANICALLY DUPLICATING OR REPRODUCING IN ANY WAY ANY PART OF THIS BOOK FOR ANY PURPOSE. •
S B N: 03-084856-3

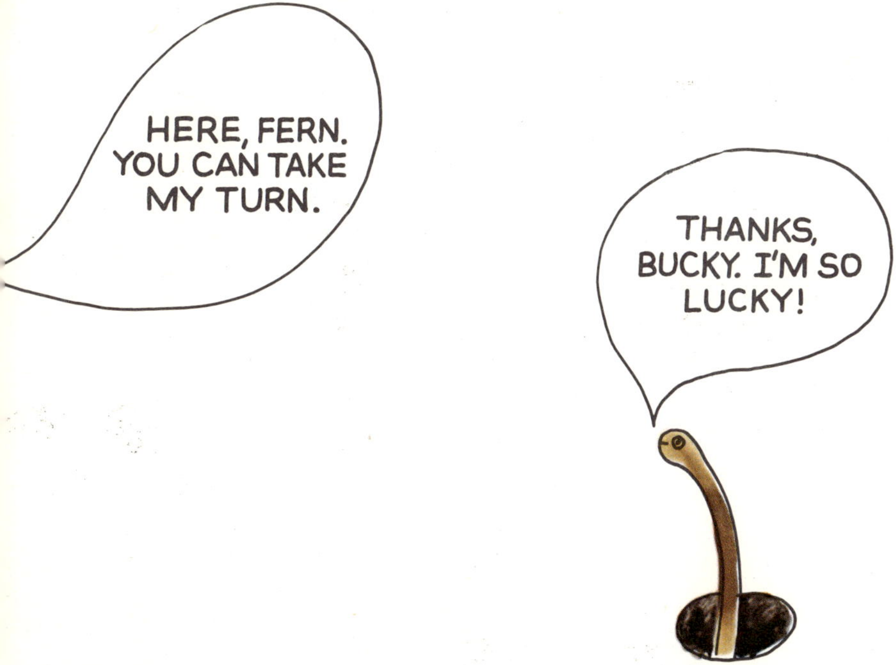

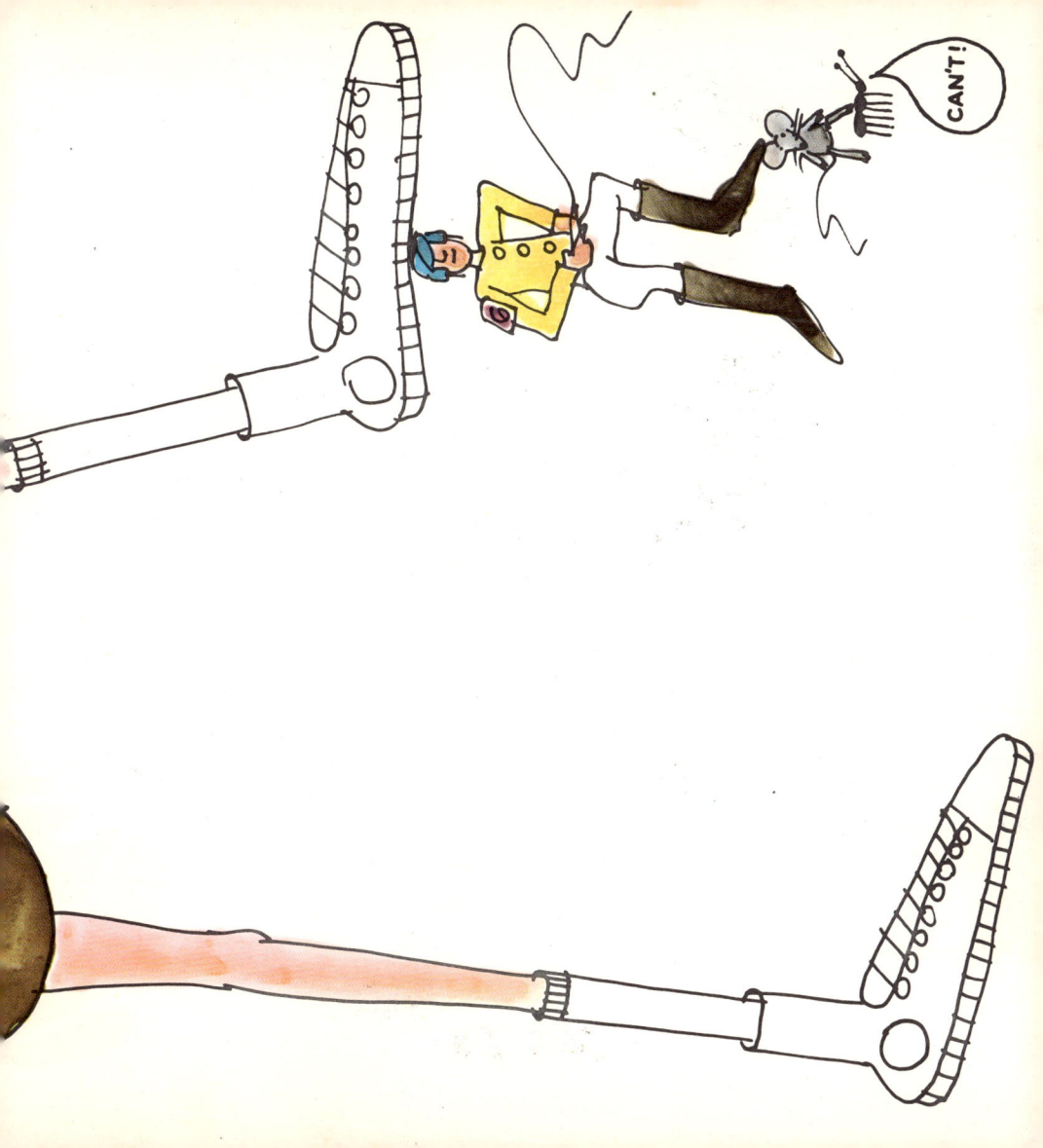